MY EMERGENCY

FUSION

ALLERGIC REACTION

By Charis Mather

BEARPORT
PUBLISHING

Minneapolis, Minnesota

Photo Credits:
Images are courtesy of Shutterstock.com.
With thanks to Getty Images, Thinkstock Photo, and iStockphoto.

Front cover – K-D-uk, Keith Homan, narikan, yusufdemirci, svtdesign, judyjump. 4–5 – Irina Strelnikova, Anton Prohorov, graficriver_icons_logo, Andrii Iemelianenko, Anatoliy Karlyuk. 6–7 – TY Lim, Akira1592, Lapina, FamVeld, Kzenon, New Africa. 8–9 – Evan Lorne, n_defender, JenJ_Payless, okskaz, Chendongshan, Eva Speshneva, Nadya_Art, robuart, Andrii Bezvershenko, Kolonko, Tanya Antusenok, Sudowoodo. 10–11 – Alexander_Safonov, olga chuprina, Lisa Kingdon, nacho roca, poltu shyamal, komokvm, stock_studio, Daria Grebenchuk. 12–13 – Medvid.com, Natty_Blissful. 14–15 – Yurii_Yarema, Sarawut Kh, Keith Homan. 16–17 – ROMAN DZIUBALO, CGN089. 18–19 – Prostock-studio, Mircea Moira, APVCTR. 20–21 – diplomedia, Mircea Moira, ESB Professional, graficriver_icons_logo, White Wolf, Chief Design, Pranch. 22–23 – Marcos Mesa Sam Wordley, Mongkolchon Akesin, Keith Homan.

Library of Congress Cataloging-in-Publication Data is available at www.loc.gov or upon request from the publisher.

ISBN: 978-1-63691-967-6 (hardcover)
ISBN: 978-1-63691-972-0 (paperback)
ISBN: 978-1-63691-977-5 (ebook)

For more information, write to Bearport Publishing, 5357 Penn Avenue South, Minneapolis, MN 55419. Printed in the United States of America.

CONTENTS

WOULD YOU KNOW WHAT TO DO?

Today, let's learn what to do in an emergency. This is when something **dangerous** is happening. What can we do if someone needs help?

Would you know what to do in an emergency?

4

People who have **serious** allergies may need help in an emergency. Allergies can affect some people a lot and other people only a little.

WHAT IS AN ALLERGIC REACTION?

Sometimes, things that are bad for us get into our bodies. When this happens, our bodies try to get rid of them.

ACHOO!

Our bodies make us sneeze and cough to get rid of bad things.

Some bodies will attack things that are not normally dangerous. We call these things allergens (AL-ur-juhnz).

Different people are affected by different allergens.

ALL ABOUT ALLERGENS

There are lots of different allergens.

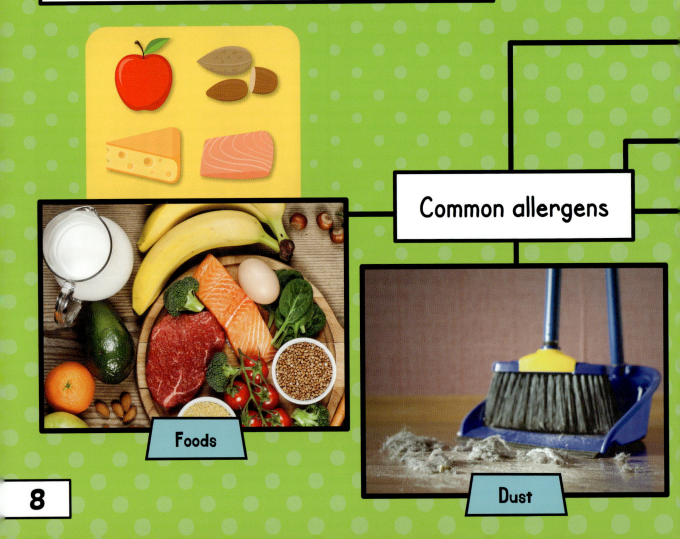

Common allergens

Foods

Dust

Drugs

Plants

Animals

When our bodies attack an allergen, it is called an allergic reaction.

HAVING A REACTION

Allergic reactions are different for everybody. What might they look like?

Itchy eyes

Sneezing

Coughing

Having a hard time breathing

Getting itchy, red skin called a **rash**

Some people have a big reaction. But for others reactions are small.

Allergic reactions can happen when you touch, eat, or breathe in an allergen. It may only take a few minutes for your body to respond.

Touching

Breathing

Eating

Even a tiny amount of an allergen can cause a reaction.

ANAPHYLACTIC SHOCK

Allergic reactions are **uncomfortable**. But most of the time they are not dangerous. However, some people have a serious reaction called anaphylactic shock (an-uh-fuh-LAK-tik shahk).

People going into shock can . . .

Have a very
bad rash

Feel sick and
dizzy

Have a body part
that is **swollen**

Look pale and
weak

Fall down and
seem asleep

These things
usually happen
quickly and
are very
dangerous.

Medicine

Most people who have a serious allergy carry **medicines** with them. Some look like big pens. They get medicine into the body very quickly.

These big pens have a few parts.

Safety cap

NEEDLE END

Needle cap

TWIST

Be careful. These pens have a needle in them. Keep the safety cap on if the pen isn't being used.

This kind of medicine can be called an EpiPen.

People who have these medicines are taught how to use them safely by a doctor.

WARNING SIGNS

If someone is about to go into shock, there might be some warning signs. Pay attention to what is happening to the person with allergies.

Are there any allergens nearby? Is the person having trouble breathing? Have they fallen down? If you see a warning sign, they might be having an allergic reaction.

WHAT CAN YOU DO?

When you see someone going into shock, you should call 911 right away. They can help in an emergency.

Tell a grown-up what is happening if there is one nearby.

18

The person at 911 will ask you some questions so they can learn what is happening. Make sure to listen carefully and answer clearly.

Tell the person at 911 someone is going into anaphylactic shock.

GETTING HELP

Ask a grown-up how to call 911. That way you'll be ready if something happens!

Call 911 only when there is an emergency.

911. What is your emergency?

Someone is going into anaphylactic shock.

I'll send help right away.

21

WHAT NEXT?

It is good to be ready for an emergency. If you know your friend has an allergy to something, be careful to stay away from that thing when you are together.

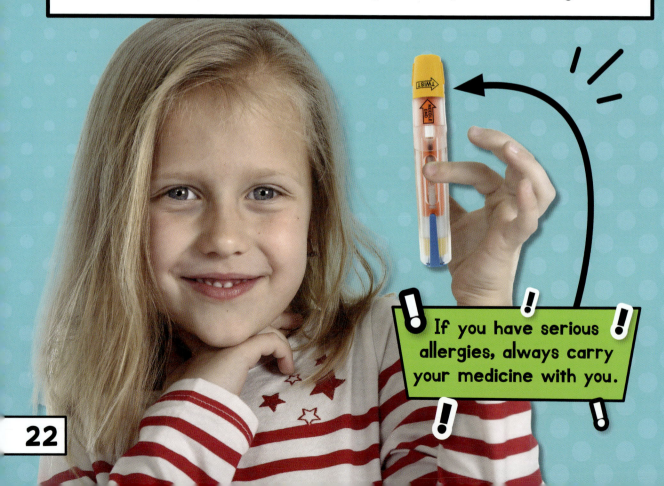

If you have serious allergies, always carry your medicine with you.

LIVING WITH ALLERGIES

Many people with allergies can live normal lives if they are on the lookout for their allergens.

GLOSSARY

dangerous involving possible harm

medicines things used or taken to fight off sickness or pain

needle a thin tube of metal that can be used to get medicine into the body

rash spots or red patches on the skin that are usually itchy or sore

serious having the possibility to be dangerous

swollen puffy or larger than something was previously

uncomfortable not feeling well or right

INDEX